What's happening?

A small church in Derby started a monthly gathering in the style of a café. The eve advertised for people who are spiritual but not religious. There is good coffee, good music and a short input around a theme each month. After four months, the community gathering at Soul Café was regularly more than 100 people.

An inner-city church in St Helen's has lunch clubs for the elderly meeting on Mondays, Wednesdays and Fridays. Last year, the church decided to offer a service of Holy Communion after each lunch club and to treat each as a separate congregation. The church added 70 communicants each week to its services.

A Methodist church in Southwell was finding that its monthly all-age worship wasn't working for anyone and it was becoming impossible to find leaders for its Junior Church. After much prayer, the church began a new weekly all-age congregation at 9.30 a.m. More than 40 people attend regularly, some of them new to the church.

Contemplative Fire was launched in September 2004 as a fresh expression of church near Aylesbury, authorized by the Diocese of Oxford's Cutting Edge Ministries. It is now emerging as a network church with small cells in Bucks, Birmingham, Bristol, Brighton and even Budapest!

Through a provision of small groups, regular gatherings for contemplative communion, pilgrimages and a major teaching programme near Oxford, Contemplative Fire seeks to provide access to the rich treasury of Christian spirituality. Core members on this journey, who are encouraged to keep a rhythm of life, are called 'Peregrini' – travelling companions on the way.

Sanctus1 was established in Manchester in 2001 in response to the large number of young professionals moving back into the city centre. Sanctus1 offers community in its weekly meetings, worship at its monthly gathering and mission in the bars of the city centre: a fresh expression of church for networked, young, urban Britain.

The Breakfast Club at All Saints in the council estates of Canterbury has been meeting for two years. It offers good food, a clothing exchange, discussion of a life issue each week and a chance to pray for one another. For the 30 or so people who come, this is their church.

A church in Haslington began Church Mice in 2003 for under fives and their families. Church Mice have a short fun time of praise including games and a story followed by refreshments and a craft activity. At 3 o'clock everyone either goes home or to school to meet their big brothers and sisters.

A new church plant in Reading has started a short all-age service on Thursday afternoons for children and parents at school pick-up time. Up to 50 come each week, 80 per cent of whom have no other church connection. The model has also worked successfully in a more traditional church setting in South London.

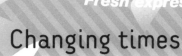

Changing times

Why are so many Christians beginning fresh expressions of church? Part of the reason is that the society around us is changing very rapidly.

- **The pattern of the week has changed.** Many people now work on Sundays. For others, Sunday is a day for sport or their only day off or essential time with families. People need opportunities for worship and community on other days.

- **The way we relate to others has changed.** People used to relate closely to where they lived. We knew our neighbours, travelled less and lived near our parents and extended family. Nowadays, relationships tend to be formed by 'networks' through our work or through our leisure. The people we know may not all live in the same place. The Church needs to learn how to relate to these significant networks as well as to particular areas.

- **Our culture has changed.** In the past, there was one recognizable 'culture' for most of our society. The churches were a central part of that culture. Now there are many different groups and subcultures. There are more television channels with smaller audiences. There are more styles of music with their own following. The Church is no longer central to this changing pattern of culture. Yet God calls us to carry the good news to all of these different cultures and groups.

- **Today, much of the British population knows less and less about Christianity** (although most people still believe in God and claim to be Christians). Signs, symbols and traditions which mean a lot within the Church are very hard for an outsider to understand. We need fresh expressions of church for those who need to begin at the very beginning.

- **Our society may be becoming less religious but it is becoming more spiritual.** People are looking for meaning and answers to life's big questions. Many are spiritual seekers. There is a rising interest in all forms of spiritual experience. Often, people do not connect this spiritual search with 'traditional' churches.

For discussion

How do these changes affect your family, your community and your church?

What other changes can you think of that are not mentioned here?

What different cultural and social groups are you aware of? Are there already any members of your church from these groups?

2

We believe . . .

It's not easy for the churches to navigate through these changing times. In the whole of Christian history, no one has faced exactly the challenges we face today. In the face of these challenges and changes, it's easy to blame others or to think that we have failed.

Blame and failure are not a good place to begin. As Christians, we need to accept that we face challenging times – and we need to remember our faith.

We believe in God who created the whole world and everyone in it. We believe that God loves the world and that God is active in the world both outside the Church and within it. Our calling as Christians is to hold firm to that faith. So our mission is to discover what God is doing in our communities now and join in.

We believe in Jesus, the Son of God, who became a man and lived among us. The Gospels tell us that Jesus always went beyond the religious communities to those at the edge of society. Jesus' life and calling was as a servant. In the same way, we are called to carry the good news about Jesus to our own communities. It is no longer enough simply to invite people to come to us and do things our way. For many, the cultural distance is too great. We need to go where people are and demonstrate God's love in action.

We believe Jesus set aside his divine power and status to become human. The Church is called to follow his lead and truly enter into other people's worlds even at the cost of some things it values.

We believe that Jesus died on the cross for all men and women. We believe that Jesus rose again and offers new life to all. The calling of the Church is to communicate the good news of Jesus' death and resurrection to everyone in a way they can understand and receive it. Often, the life of the Church itself may also involve death and resurrection as we seek to follow Jesus. We trust that God will bring about new ways from the old.

We believe that God sends the Holy Spirit on the Church in every generation to equip us for mission. The Spirit makes us restless to carry the gospel to new places. The Spirit guides us in the journey we must take. The Spirit breathes life into the different fresh expressions of church.

We believe that the Church in every generation is called to be one (across the world and all time), holy (dedicated to God), catholic (for the whole world) and apostolic (founded on the apostles' teaching and sent by God in mission). But there are many different ways we can meet together; many different ways to worship God; many different ways to form community; many different ways to serve society and share faith.

For discussion

What do you think God is doing in your own community outside the Church?

What might we have to set aside to enter the culture of people beyond the churches?

How is the Spirit making you restless to carry the gospel to new places?

Learning to be a both-and Church

Does all of this mean the Church has to abandon what we are doing and all the traditions we love? Not at all!

All the research suggests that, when done well, the traditional forms of church are still helpful and meaningful for up to 40 per cent of the population. This is a wonderful mission field. We need to continue to develop and grow the Church as it is. There are many ways to do this:

- through becoming a more welcoming and open community
- through offering ways for all ages to learn about faith
- through worship and preaching that have depth and relevance
- through inviting people into life-changing discipleship and service

However, research also tells us that at least 60 per cent of the UK population finds it difficult to connect with the Church as it is in terms of our normal Sunday worship. Many believe in God. Many are searching for spiritual meaning. They are not beyond God's love or the Christian gospel. However it is no longer enough for churches simply to say: 'Come to us and be church this way'. We need to go to where people are and sow the seed of the gospel in new ways.

60% of the UK population find it difficult to connect with the Church

We therefore need to develop a mixed economy church. Both-and means traditional churches alongside many different fresh expressions of church for a changing world, with all of them facing outwards to others.

In 2004 the Church of England produced a report called *Mission-shaped Church: church planting and fresh expressions of church in a changing culture*.

The report was unanimously commended by the General Synod in February 2004 and 15,000 copies were sold in the first year. The report has been widely discussed at national and diocesan level and is being put into practice by many dioceses.

The Methodist Church was represented on the Working Party that produced the report and in 2005 the Methodist Conference agreed a new set of priorities, which include:

- developing confidence in evangelism and in the capacity to speak of God and faith in ways that make sense to all involved;

- encouraging fresh ways of being church.

Later in 2004 the Archbishops, with the support of the Methodist Council, set up a new initiative, Fresh Expressions. The aim of Fresh Expressions is to resource mission through fresh expressions of church life in every place.

Fresh Expressions works in partnership with the churches at national level, in dioceses and districts and with a number of mission agencies including Church Army, Anglican Church Planting Initiatives, the Church Mission Society, New Way and the Church Pastoral Aid Society.

The **Methodist** Church   freshexpressions

For discussion

Do you agree with this both-and direction for the future?

What can be done to make your own church more mission-shaped?

What needs to be done locally to put this both-and thinking into practice?

Changes are being introduced at national level to help local churches develop fresh expressions of church.

- Resources are being made available to dioceses through the Church Commissioners and to districts and circuits through changes in the rules for Circuit and District Advance Funds.

- A new Pastoral Measure for the Church of England was approved by General Synod in 2004 and is now at committee stage to enable the recognition of new churches alongside parishes.

- Changes are being made to the selection and training for ordained ministry to encourage and equip pioneer ministers.

- Dioceses and districts are working together as an expression of the Covenant to share resources and best practice. Local forums are meeting to share news of what is happening and to develop local training.

- Many dioceses and some districts and circuits have already established mission funds for new initiatives and have appointed staff to encourage and facilitate fresh expressions of church.

- Fresh Expressions and its partner agencies are offering training to every diocese and district in 2006.

All of these new ventures are being supported in prayer. The Methodist Church has set aside this Conference Year as a year when Methodists 'Pray without Ceasing' (http://www.praywithoutceasing.org.uk).

Fresh expressions in every place . . .

The report, *Mission-shaped Church*, describes twelve different categories of fresh expressions of church.

In February 2005 the Fresh Expressions web site was launched. At the centre of the web site is a national online directory of fresh expressions of church. There are already hundreds of fresh expressions on the web site. Each one tells a story of Christians reaching out to their communities. There are stories from urban and rural backgrounds, from every part of the country and based in churches of every tradition. Some examples are started by a local church; others by local churches working together in deaneries or circuits; others by dioceses or districts.

York: A large church in the centre of York began a Sunday morning service in a local gym for those on the edge of church life. Many people combine going to the gym with attending the church. The congregation grew to more than 70 within a few months.

re:generation is a youth-orientated church plant within the Romford Methodist Circuit. It began in September 2004 and seeks to relate to the need and visions of the emerging generation of Christian and non-Christian young people today. Two out of every four services are followed by an hour and a half of quality social time.

Sunday 4.6 A deanery evangelist works with 21 small, mainly elderly congregations in rural Devon. She has started a new monthly interdenominational service on Sunday afternoons targeted at adults and older people. Nine months on, Sunday 4.6 has a sizeable group attending on a regular basis including a significant number who were not previously churchgoers.

Mind the Gap started in 2001 in the Newcastle District. It's a new kind of cell church aimed at the 18s–40s in Gateshead. There are regular cell meetings, a monthly celebration on a Sunday evening, Alpha courses and seeker events.

3six5 is a missional congregation focused on supporting Christian lifestyle and witness. The emphasis is on church as a dispersed people, rather than a people gathered in a building. The new initiative began in 2001 in Kingston-on-Thames. Members meet weekly for a study session following the principles of base ecclesial communities and fortnightly for worship together on Saturday teatime.

Fellowship @ Grannies meets in a tea shop in Cotgrave, Nottinghamshire, every Thursday evening. It began as an after-Alpha group and is now meeting regularly for worship and fellowship.

The Malt Cross is a café bar in the city centre of Nottingham. The intention is for it to be a safe place in the city to explore life and expand community through relational space, creative space, thinking space and sacred space. It's more of a friary than a church and is developing a dispersed community of believers.

Churches in Bridlington, Northampton, Twickenham and Ashford have each started and registered several different fresh expressions of church – new initiatives serving different sections of their community.

The Net in Huddersfield began in 2001 particularly through the support of the Bishop's staff. It's a new network church for people with no experience of church life.

Developing fresh expressions of church is not just a bright idea from the centre or a plan to somehow manage ourselves out of decline. It is a response in our generation to the call of Jesus to make disciples and to take the gospel to every place. It must therefore begin and continue in prayer and listening to the Spirit.

We are all learning together how to engage in mission in this way. We need courage and commitment but also humility to listen to the wider community outside the church to find out what God is doing there. No one has all the answers. All of us have something to contribute to the learning of the whole church.

'When Jesus saw the crowds, he had compassion for them, because they were like sheep without a shepherd. Then he said to his disciples, "The harvest is plentiful but the labourers are few: therefore ask the Lord of the harvest to send out labourers into his harvest."'

Matthew 9.36-37

For discussion

How do you respond to these stories?

What do you know of any fresh expressions of church near to where you live?

Do they spark any ideas for your own situation?

How do we start?

There is no single way to start a fresh expression of church. The whole Church is learning about how to do this. The following is a 'rough guide' to the process you might follow, but it needs to be adapted locally. There are resources and ideas for each stage on the fresh expressions web site.

1. Build mission-centred values at the heart of the Church as it is

Is there a desire to share in God's mission, to serve the community, to welcome others and to reach out to new communities? Is there an emphasis on the call of every Christian to service and discipleship? Is there an awareness of the Spirit's work, equipping the Church for mission?

2. Listen, pray and form vision

Listen to and pray for your local communities and culture both locally around the church building and more widely. This may involve using some mission audit materials prepared to help churches get to know their communities. What is God doing? Listen to what God is saying to you. Where does God call you to work? Is there a calling to focus on what you are already doing? Is there a calling to begin something new? For most churches, this will be both-and.

3. Prune a little

Many churches are busy places. Not all of our structures or meetings are necessary. To create space and energy for mission, we need to learn to travel light. Are there places you can simplify church life to make more space and release gifts and energy for something new? Make sure you don't simply get stuck here and never move on to the mission!

4. Form a team

This will never be a solo enterprise. Look to establish a core team of people who can carry the project forward. The team will need the right support: connexion from within the church, prayer, the right training and mission accompaniment for the early years of the project. As they engage with the context they will need to learn the characteristics and values of the culture and have the wisdom to let the fresh expression be shaped by what they find in the mission process.

5. Feed your imagination

Get to know what is happening in other places. Research them online. Send people out to visit fresh expressions in your area. Go to some training events. Find out all you can about the different things God is doing.

6. Explore partnerships

Sometimes churches will have the resources to do something new on their own. Sometimes you will need to work together with other churches across an area. Build good links and work together – but keep the structures simple. For some fresh expressions there will be issues of permission to get right with church authorities and structures. Sometimes partnerships will be with non-church groups such as schools or government agencies.

7. Form community

Most fresh expressions of church begin by forming new communities among different groups of people with something in common. Loving service normally comes before a worship service. Once there is community, there is often an opportunity to introduce learning about the Christian faith and, in time, worship that speaks to the culture.

8. Allow growth to maturity

Fresh expressions need time and space to grow in their own way. Some will be for a time, others are long-term projects. All will need the grace, support and space to grow to maturity over several years. Like watching over children as they grow, parenting can be demanding. The aim is to raise healthy, mature adults.

9. Maintain connexion

It is vital that there are excellent links of connexion between different parts of the church. This needs thinking through in advance. It will be different for a local fresh expression attached to an existing parish; for one attached to a circuit or deanery or for a venture across a whole town. There are lots of good models emerging.

10. Share what you are doing

The whole church is learning how to do this and no one has all the answers. Help us learn. Register what you are doing on the fresh expressions web site. Tell the story locally. Be prepared to help others get started.

> **'If "church" is what happens when people encounter the Risen Jesus and commit themselves to sustaining and deepening that encounter in their encounter with each other, there is plenty of theological room for diversity of rhythm and style, so long as we have ways of identifying the same living Christ at the heart of every expression of Christian life in common.'**
>
> Archbishop Rowan Williams,
> from the Preface to *Mission-shaped Church*

For discussion

Are you ready and willing to move forward in establishing a fresh expression? Decide what you need to do in the next month, in the next six months and in the next year.

Where to get help

Fresh Expressions is committed to encouraging fresh expressions of church in every diocese and district over the next four years.

Go to **www.freshexpressions.org.uk** for:

- the online directory and hundreds of examples;
- details of training events happening soon;
- additional resources to support this booklet including ideas for reading, resource sheets and online training;
- downloadable Powerpoint presentations and details of DVD resources;
- training events that can be arranged for your circuit or deanery.

We have produced a tabloid newspaper with lots of stories of fresh expressions for free distribution this autumn. For copies for your congregation and for other enquiries email: **contact@freshexpressions.org.uk** or write to Fresh Expressions, 15 Fyfield Road, Oxford, OX2 6QE.

The Church Army

The Church Army's Sheffield Centre was started in order to research this area for the wider church.

Go to our web site: **www.encountersontheedge.org.uk** for:

- details of the *Encounters on the Edge* series – over 25 extended stories highlight lessons in practice about fresh expressions of church over a wide range of contexts;
- downloadable Word files and Powerpoint presentations about different aspects of Mission-shaped Church and other research into today's mission;
- a contact person who can offer email-based consultancy for those considering or leading a fresh expression of church;
- a contact person running our database who handles queries for information and examples;
- Details of university-validated block weeks, at the Church Army College in Sheffield, connected to *Mission-shaped Church* issues.

In some cases Church Army can partner a sending church to deploy a leader for a prospective fresh expression of church. Contact **www.churcharmy.org.uk**

How to use this booklet

In a Church Council meeting, small group or special open meeting for the congregation

Preparation

Buy enough copies for everyone at the meeting and send them out in advance. The people leading the meeting should also look at the Mission-shaped Church report and do some research on what is happening locally. The outline below links the material with different chapters of the report. You may also want to have some additional resources to take away.

Every church and small group is different and will vary in their starting point so you will need to adapt this outline. The first timings are based on a 90-minute meeting. There is certainly material for an away day or for several meetings.

Stories [15 minutes] MSC 4

Introduce the evening and begin with some stories taken from the booklet or from local research. How do you respond to them?

Changing times [15 minutes] MSC 1

Introduce the section on changing times either with a brief overview or using Powerpoint or OHP slides and focus on the questions for discussion.

We believe [15 minutes] MSC 5

Ask the group to divide into twos and threes and look at the 'We believe . . .' section. How do they respond to the ideas there? Are there any questions to ask as a whole group?

Learning to be a both-and Church [10 minutes] MSC 7

Lead a plenary discussion. What is the priority for your own church and for you at this time – doing traditional church more effectively or beginning a fresh expression (or is it both)?

How do we start? [15 minutes] MSC 6

Give a short overview of the eight steps to be followed and look together at the final questions for discussion.

Prayer together [10 minutes]

Commit all of your discussion and planning and your local community to God in prayer.

For a series of four meetings

We suggest the following themes for each week:

1. Changing times
2. We believe
3. Learning to be a both-and Church
4. Getting started

For each meeting, you may like to use the following structure:

- Group sharing around the reading and research you have done
- A short input summarizing the main theme of the evening
- Focus on the questions for discussion

You will find additional support material including Powerpoint presentations and Bible studies on the Fresh Expressions web site: **www.freshexpressions.org.uk/resources/movingon**

'The Spirit is seeking to make the Church into the vibrant vehicle of God's tomorrow, not the museum piece of yesterday.'

The Revd Tom Stuckey,
President of the
Methodist Conference